Communities: Alike and Different

by Donna Foley

Editorial Offices: Glenview, Illinois • Parsippany, New Jersey • New York, New York
Sales Offices: Needham, Massachusetts • Duluth, Georgia • Glenview, Illinois
Coppell, Texas • Ontario, California • Mesa, Arizona

Communities are alike and different in many ways. Communities are made up of neighborhoods, or places where people live and work together. Some communities have different neighborhoods crowded into small areas. Each **community** uses land differently and creates neighborhoods for the people living there. There are three types of communities.

Urban communities have a city. A city is a very large community with many different neighborhoods close together.

Urban neighborhoods are crowded and have many buildings. Some urban neighborhoods have their own identity, such as Chinatown or Little Italy. Other urban neighborhoods have many businesses. People usually live in apartment buildings in urban neighborhoods.

Urban communities bring many different types of cultures together.

Suburbs are communities near cities. They have houses for families to live in. Many people who work in the city live in the suburbs. A **suburb** is sometimes called a town. A suburb usually has a town center with places to shop. There may be many neighborhoods around the town center.

Rural communities have a lot of open space. Rural communities are very spread out over the land. Many rural areas have farms with land to grow crops or raise animals. People in rural communities usually live and work on farms. There are not many shops in rural communities. People usually have to drive to town to shop.

In urban communities, people live in neighborhoods that have lots of apartment buildings. Many people and families live in each apartment building. People sometimes walk down the hall to visit their neighbors. Families usually do not have their own yards. In urban neighborhoods some families make small gardens on their balconies by planting flowers and vegetables in flower boxes.

In suburban communities, people live in neighborhoods with many houses near each other. They can walk to their neighbor's house for a visit. Their houses usually have trees and yards around them. Some families plant flowers or vegetable gardens. There is land to grow all kinds of things.

In rural communities there is usually a lot of room between houses. Neighbors may not live close to one another. People sometimes need to drive if they want to visit a neighbor.

In urban communities, neighborhoods are very crowded and busy. There are many stores and restaurants in urban neighborhoods. People shop near their apartments and can sometimes walk to the market to buy food.

Urban communities also have many cultural centers and parks. People can visit museums and libraries.

In suburban communities the town center may be a meeting place for people. People usually walk or drive a short distance to the town center. People go to town to shop. There may be a market, small shops, and a few restaurants. Families and friends meet to spend time together.

There are also shopping malls near the suburbs. The shopping malls have many types of stores. People go to shopping malls to buy things they cannot find in town.

In rural communities the town center is very small. People need to drive to town. There is usually a market and only a few shops. There are a few meeting places for friends and families.

In rural communities, families and friends spend more time together at home. People need to visit bigger towns and cities to shop, eat out, or visit a museum.

In urban communities, people move quickly from place to place. Many people use public transportation. People take buses or subways to travel to places in the city.

In urban neighborhoods many people walk and may not drive a car. Their neighborhoods are too crowded for parking spaces. Driving in the city can be slow because there is a lot of traffic.

In suburban communities many people use cars for transportation. Streets in suburban communities have less traffic than city streets, so it is easier to drive from place to place. Other people ride bicycles or walk.

There are also buses in suburban communities, but there are usually fewer buses than in urban communities. Suburbs have many buses in the morning and late afternoon. People use these buses to get to work and school.

Many people in suburbs live far from where they work. Many people work in a city near their town. Many towns have train stations. People take the trains to the city.

In rural communities, people use cars to travel from place to place. People usually live too far away from places to walk. Some people ride bicycles.

Buses usually do not travel from neighborhood to neighborhood in rural communities. People can take a bus from the town center to other towns or to the city. There are usually only a few buses that run each day. People may have to plan their travel around the bus schedule.

Communities are the same in many ways. Some have neighborhoods with people and families. People live, work, and travel in communities. People are often connected to one another in their communities.

Communities are different in many ways. Communities use land differently for neighborhoods. Some communities have neighborhoods with many people. Some communities have neighborhoods with people living near each other and working in other communities. Communities are special places to live!

Glossary

community a place that is made up of many neighborhoods

rural an area with small communities and open space

suburb a type of community that is located near a city

urban an area that has a city